Disney · PIXAR

FINDING NEMO

SWIM, SLITHER, AND SOAR
ALL ABOUT SEA TURTLES, SNAKES, BIRDS, AND MORE!
by Sharon Katz Cooper

Scholastic Inc.
New York · Toronto · London · Auckland · Sydney
Mexico City · New Delhi · Hong Kong · Buenos Aires

Cover Designer: Rocco Melillo
Interior Designer: Rocco Melillo, Julia Sarno
Interior illustrations: Yancey Labat

Published by Scholastic Inc., 557 Broadway, New York, NY 10012,
by arrangement with Disney Licensed Publishing. SCHOLASTIC and associated
logos are trademarks and/or registered trademarks of Scholastic Inc.

ISBN 0-439-80885-5

12 11 10 9 8 7 6 5 4 3 2 1   5 6 7 8 9 10/0

Printed in the U.S.A.
First Scholastic printing, September 2005

Table of Contents

Introduction: Let's Take a Dive & Soar in the Sky!.... 8

Chapter 1: Reptile Files........................ 10

Chapter 2: Sea Turtles, Dude!.................. 12

Chapter 3: Snakes in the Sea 19

Fishy Fun: What's Wrong in the Water?. 22

Chapter 4: A Bird's Life...................... 23

Chapter 5: Party with the Penguins! 25

Chapter 6: Big-Billed Birds 29

Chapter 7: Seagulls by the Seashore 31

Chapter 8: The Biggest Flying Bird of All 33

Fishy Fun: Bird Brain! 35

Show-and-Tell with Ornithologist, Betty Anne Schreiber..... 36

School's Out!................................ 37

Nemo's Answer Page 38

Nemo
clown fish

Let's take a Dive & soar in the SKY!

HI, I'm Nemo! Welcome back to Undersea School! Are you ready to learn about some of my scaly and feathered friends? The ocean is full of cool creatures—and they're not all fish! We'll check out reptiles, like our sea turtle friends, Crush and Squirt, and the world of seabirds, including Nigel and those loud seagulls. You'll meet all kinds of cool animals in this book, including:

- **eight kinds of sea turtles,**

- **snakes that are super-poisonous,**

- **penguins that "fly" underwater,**

- **and a seabird with the largest wingspan in the world!**

8

We'll have a great time as we ride ocean currents, follow turtle babies from the beach to the sea, and find out where seabirds live and what they like to eat.

Did you know that sea turtles:

- **breathe air, just like you,**

- **swim thousands of miles (that's really, really far!),**

- **and lay eggs in the sand?**

Did you ever think of birds as ocean animals? Well, guess what...some are! We'll look at seabirds that:

- **never fly.**

- **steal food from other birds.**

- **like to swallow rocks.**

- **scoop up fish in a large pouch.**

So, put on your flippers (and get your wings ready!)...we're about to dive into some awesome undersea adventures!

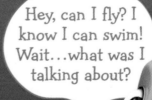

Whoa! Turtles are totally cool, dude!

squirt
sea turtle

Hey, can I fly? I know I can swim! Wait...what was I talking about?

Dory
blue tang

9

Chapter 1: Reptile Files

Let's swim on over for a visit with our scaly friends, the *reptiles*! Reptiles are a lot cooler than you may think. They're *ectothermic* (ECK-toh-ther-mik), which means they're cold blooded, just like me and other fish. Reptiles are also vertebrates (VER-tuh-bruhts), which means they have backbones. But unlike fish, they have lungs instead of gills.

Meet the Marine Reptiles

You may already know some land reptiles: snakes, tortoises, iguanas, lizards, and alligators. But marine reptiles are different. They spend most of their lives in the water and come up from time to time to breathe air. And since they can't make their own body heat, almost all marine reptiles live in warm, tropical waters.

Even though we need to come up for air, we can stay under water for a long time—sometimes for as long as five hours!

green sea turtles

So, who are my sea-living reptile friends? There are eight different kinds of sea turtles. We'll learn more about them in the next chapter!

Clowning Around!

Q: What kind of tiles wouldn't look good on your kitchen walls?

A: *Rep*-tiles!

Marlin
clown fish

banded sea snake

There are about 60 different kinds of sea snakes. They are way cool and way poisonous!

marine iguana

There's one kind of marine lizard: the marine iguana. We won't talk a lot about them, but they're interesting because they eat plants instead of animals. Good news for us fishies!

Okay, dude—I'm going to let Crush tell you all about sea turtles in the next chapter. See you later!

That's a Mouthful, Mate!

Hello there, mate! Let's take a bite out of the word: *ectothermic*. Animals that are ectothermic can't make their own body heat. That means their temperature is pretty close to the air or water around them. Birds and mammals, like you, are *endothermic* (EN-doh-ther-mik). That means they make their own heat.

BRUCE
great white shark

Chapter 2: Sea Turtles, Dude!

crush
sea turtle

Hey, little dude!
I'm Crush, the sea turtle. I thought I'd cruise on over from the EAC to tell you all about me and my totally awesome turtle friends. Are you ready for some serious thrills? Then grab shell, dude, and let's go!

The Truth About Turtles

Sea turtles have large shells and streamlined shapes, which make us super-cool and super-fast swimmers. Our totally awesome cousins, the land turtles, can pull their heads and legs into their shells, but sea turtles can't do that. Hey, we can't all be the same! Let's swim to the next page for a look at one of my fellow green sea turtles.

Eyelids & Salt Gland

We have two big eyelids that protect our eyes. We also have a salt gland located right behind our eyes. That's a little organ that helps us get rid of salt from the seawater. This gland empties out in our eyes, so it makes us look like we're crying. But don't worry, dude, we're totally happy!

Shell

We have big, bony shells to protect our bodies. Almost all sea turtles have a layer of hard *scutes* (SKOOTS) or horny plates that cover their shells. Scientists often identify turtles by the number and pattern of scutes on their shells.

Flippers

Unlike our land cousins, we've got the most excellent swimming flippers. Our front flippers work like large paddles to help us push through the water, while our rear flippers help us steer.

That's a Mouthful, Mate!

Scutes are hard bony plates made of a flexible material called cartilage. You have cartilage in your nose and ears.

Chum
mako shark

The Great Eight

Sea turtles are in a big group of reptiles that includes all turtles and big tortoises. Scientists divide sea turtles into two families: one with scutes, and the other without scutes. There's only one kind of turtle in that second group, dude—the leatherback. More about this excellent guy later.

There are eight kinds of sea turtles. There's the green sea turtle (that's me and Squirt), the black sea turtle, the loggerhead sea turtle, Kemp's ridley sea turtle, the olive ridley sea turtle, the hawksbill sea turtle, the flatback sea turtle, and the totally righteous leatherback sea turtle.

Here they all are, little dude. Swim on over and say hello!

green sea turtle

black sea turtle

loggerhead sea turtle

Kemp's ridley sea turtle

olive ridley sea turtle

hawksbill sea turtle

flatback sea turtle

leatherback sea turtle

We all like to be super comfortable, so we live in warm waters all over the world. Hawksbill and ridleys are as small as 21 inches (53 cm) long, while the leatherback can grow to six feet (1.8 m) long and weigh 1,100 pounds (499 kg)! That guy's a monster! I call him Leather-man.

Something's Fishy

Pssst! Hey, kid! Wanna know more about Crush's pal, Leather-man? Leatherback turtles have thick and oily skin, instead of scutes like other sea turtles. Their skin protects them and keeps them warm, so leatherbacks can go where it's colder. Not bad, eh?

Gill
moorish idol

CLOWNING AROUND!

Q: What did the mother turtle say to the baby turtle?

A: Oh, you're so *scute!*

CRUISIN' ALONG

When some of us sea turtles get hungry, we migrate! Migrate means to move from one place to another to find food or a new place to live. We migrate from breeding areas, where we mate and lay eggs, to feeding areas, where we eat a lot of awesome food! Some groups of sea turtles travel thousands of miles. My cousin, Leather-man, wins the long-distance award. These righteous dudes swim more than 3,000 miles (4,828 km) from the beaches, where they make their nests, to cooler waters, where they find their food. Dude, what a wipeout!

leatherback turtle

C'mon Leather-man, just keep swimming, just keep swimming...

Dude, What's for Dinner?

hawksbill turtle eating a sponge

Sea turtles eat lots of different stuff, man. Green and black sea turtles generally eat sea grasses and algae. All that green stuff gives us the vitamins we need to stay healthy. Loggerhead and ridley turtles eat crabs, lobsters, shrimp, jellyfish, and some green plants. Hawksbills eat sponges, shrimp, and squid. Leatherbacks eat jellyfish and other soft animals.

Scientists think flatbacks eat seaweed, cuttlefish, and sea cucumbers. Yum— that sounds like a good salad!

And guess what? We do all this eating without any teeth. That's right—totally zero teeth, dude! We don't need them because we just chomp down and swallow. It totally rocks!

loggerhead turtle eating a spiny lobster

Leather-man can dive more than 1,000 feet (304.8 m) deep looking for jellyfish! Cool!

CLOWNING AROUND!

Q: Why was the sea turtle afraid of his shell?

A: Because it followed him everywhere!

Turtle Babies!

When female turtles are ready to lay eggs, they haul up onto the beach and make a nest at night. They dig holes in the sand and then lay between 50 to 200 eggs. Talk about hard work! Those eggs are about the size of Ping-Pong balls and have soft shells. Leatherback turtle eggs are bigger. After the female turtles lay their eggs, they cover them with sand to protect them from predators. Then the females go back to the water, leaving the eggs behind.

leatherback sea turtle eggs

green sea turtle hatchlings

After a few months, the little dudes (or hatchlings) are ready to hatch. They use a little temporary tooth to break open their shells and dig their way out of the sand. When it's dark, they pop their little heads out of their nests, take a look around, and make a mad dash for the water. There are lots of animals on the beach that want to eat them, so they have to be super-careful! Go, little dudes, go!

You just did some awesome swimming and learned a lot about sea turtles. You totally rock! Nemo's on his way back, so I'm going to say, 'koo-koo-ka-choo,' catch ya' in a few!

18

Chapter 3: Snakes in the Sea

Hey, it's me, Nemo, again! I hope you and Crush had a totally awesome time with the sea turtles. Now it's time to take a swim with the *sea snakes*!

Take a Deep Breath!

Even though they may look like eels (which are fish), sea snakes are reptiles. And like all reptiles, sea snakes breathe air through lungs. They can close off their noses so they don't breathe in water while they're swimming! And some of them can absorb oxygen from the water by swallowing seawater and then spitting it out. Pretty cool, huh?

leaf-scaled
sea snake

Open Wide!

Since sea snakes need to breathe air, they live in shallow water where it's easy to come up to the surface. In this shallow water, sea snakes search for fish, fish eggs, and eels as tasty treats. A sea snake can open its mouth wide enough to swallow a fish more than twice the size of its neck!

Sea snakes are pretty small, but did you know they're related to cobras— those big, poisonous land snakes? Yikes!

Tad
butterfly fish

perfectly poisonous

Sea snakes have the most toxic, or most poisonous, venom of all the snakes in the world! The moment a sea snake sinks its sharp little fangs into its prey (usually a fish), its venom stuns the prey and keeps it from swimming away. Then the snake gobbles it up! Without their venom, snakes would have a difficult time catching their food. The fish they usually eat could easily escape into tiny holes in rocks or seaweed.

sea snake feeding

slippery characters

Now that you know all about sea snakes, let's meet some of them. Don't worry, we won't get too close! C'mon—let's-s-s s-s-swim like a s-s-snake!

CLOWNING AROUND!

Q: What's the best thing about sea snakes?

A: They've got *poison*-ality!

yellow-bellied sea snake

One of the most common sea snakes is the yellow-bellied sea snake. It lives in the Pacific Ocean along the California coast and all the way down to South America. Yellow-bellied snakes usually float along with the currents and stay together in big groups. Fish that happen to swim up underneath one of these groups get gobbled up.

The olive sea snake can grow to about six feet (1.8 m)—it's one of the largest venomous sea snakes. It can be found in the Great Barrier Reef in Australia. Like most sea snakes, the olive sea snake has a flattened tail, which helps it to swim.

olive sea snake

Hello, little sea snake! I live in Australia, too. Want to go s-s-swiming together?

Dory! Stop talking to that sea snake—it's poisonous!

The bands on a banded sea snake alert other animals that it's very poisonous. Lots of animals that are poisonous have bands or stripes on them—like bees, for example.

banded sea snake

turtlehead sea snake

Turtlehead sea snakes are one of my favorite sea snakes! That's because they're not poisonous. Since they pretty much eat only fish eggs, they don't need venom to stun fast moving prey.

Are your ready to s-s-slip away from these s-s-snakes for some s-s-super Fishy Fun? Let's go!

FISHY FUN: What's Wrong in the Water?

This underwater scene is looking a little fishy! There are six strange things in the picture below. Can you find them all? (Here's a hint: Take a close look at all the animals and what they're doing!)

(When you're done, check your answers on page 38.)

Chapter 4: A Bird's Life

It's time to take flight! We're going to fly up, up, and away with some of my feathered friends—the *seabirds*. Even though many birds fly in the sky rather than swim in the sea, there are a whole bunch of birds that spend most of their time on or near the ocean. Nigel will be joining us in a moment, but first let's take a closer look at what makes a bird a bird!

All About Birds

Before we start soaring with seabirds, let's find out the basic characteristics of all birds.

Beak
Birds have beaks or bills for their mouths. If you were to take a look inside a bird's beak (*blech!* bird breath stinks!), you'd see that birds don't have teeth.

Backbone
Birds are vertebrates, just like you. Many birds have hollow bones so they don't weigh much. Being lightweight makes it easier to fly.

Feathers
All birds have feathers. They're the only group of animals in the world that do! Feathers come in many sizes and colors and help keep a bird warm and protected.

Wings
Most birds use their wings to fly, but some of them use their wings to swim instead, like penguins! (We'll learn more about them on pages 25-28.)

Preening Gland
The preening gland is a little organ at the base of the tail that makes a substance similar to wax or oil. Birds can spread this waxy stuff on their bodies to make themselves waterproof!

super seabirds

Hello there! I'm Nigel and I'm a kind of seabird called a pelican. Most seabirds have all of the general bird characteristics on page 23, but their bodies may look a little different than the birds you see mainly on land. Let's fly on over and take a closer look at a seabird!

Nigel
pelican

Large Bill
Many seabirds have special kinds of bills for eating fish or other ocean animals. Pelicans have big bills for scooping up their fishy dinners. Other birds have very sharp beaks like spears for stabbing fish.

Salt Gland
Most seabirds have a salt gland. Since they live in the ocean, seabirds have to drink salt water. But then they need a way to get that salt out of their bodies, since a bird's body—like yours—can't take too much salt. The salt gland gathers up the salt from the bird's body and then the bird can sneeze it out!

Webbed Feet
A lot of seabirds have webbed feet. They help them swim and paddle in the water.

Layer of Fat
Most seabirds have a lot of fat on their bodies to keep them warm and help them float in the water.

Now that you know all about seabirds, are you ready to meet some of them? In the next few chapters, we'll visit a whole bunch of my fellow feathered friends. The first stop on our journey: penguin paradise!

Chapter 5: Party with the Penguins!

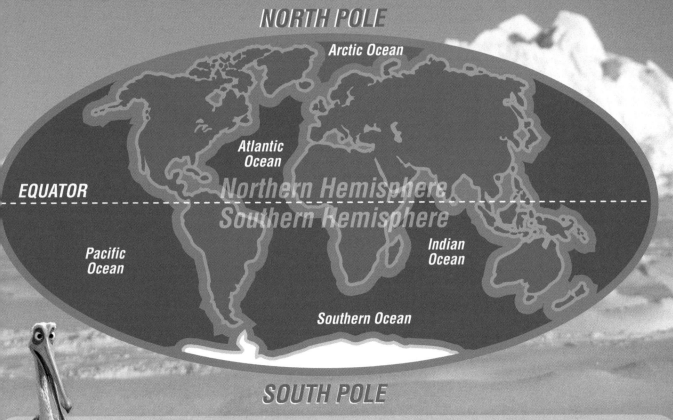

NORTH POLE

Arctic Ocean

Atlantic Ocean

EQUATOR

Northern Hemisphere
Southern Hemisphere

Indian Ocean

Pacific Ocean

Southern Ocean

SOUTH POLE

Brrrrrr! It sure is cold here! We're in the South Pole—home of the penguins. Did you know that there are 17 different kinds of penguins? They all live in the Southern hemisphere (the bottom half of the earth). Penguins don't live anywhere near the North Pole where polar bears live. One penguin, the Galápagos penguin, lives near the equator (the imaginary line around the earth's "waist" that divides the Northern and Southern hemispheres). But the water there is still really cold. Penguins are built for cold weather. They have a lot of fat under their skin, which keeps them nice and toasty!

25

No Flying Allowed!

Penguins don't fly, and they look a little silly when they walk on land or ice. But penguins are excellent swimmers! So, it's a good thing that penguins don't spend a lot of time on land. They usually only come ashore to find a mate, have babies, and *molt*. When they're on land, penguins move about by waddling very slowly. Their short, stubby tails help keep them balanced.

That's a Mouthful, Mate!

When penguins or other seabirds *molt*, they lose their old feathers and grow back new ones. This can take about three to four weeks. While penguins molt, they can't go out to sea to find food. They have to wait for their waterproof feathers to grow back in. So they get pretty hungry!

anchor
hammerhead
shark

emperor
penguin

26

Swim, Birdie, Swim!

Penguins may not fly in the air, but they sure look like they fly underwater. Penguins use their wings like flippers and their webbed feet like paddles for pushing through the water. They also have very dense and oily feathers to protect their bodies and make them smooth for some very fast swimming!

little blue penguins

Some kinds of penguins are small, like the little blue penguin. It grows to only about one foot (30.5 cm) tall. Little blue penguins live along the coasts of New Zealand and Australia. They make their nests in sandy burrows and eat fish, squid, and crabs.

Emperor penguins live in Antarctica and are the largest of all the penguins. They can grow to about four feet (122 cm) tall. Emperor penguin babies (or chicks) develop in their eggs for about two months. We'll learn more about them on page 28.

emperor penguins

Rockhoppers live on the rocky coasts of South America, where they build nests of stones and grasses. They lay two eggs, but only take care of the larger one.

rockhopper penguin

27

macaroni penguin

Macaroni penguins have bright yellow feathers on the tops of their heads—kind of like a fancy hat! They live in the Antarctic islands and the southern tips of South America and Africa.

adélie penguins

Adélie penguins are the smallest of the penguins that live on Antarctica. They grow to about a little more than two feet (61 cm) tall. Adélies live on rocky beaches and stay in groups of thousands!

Baby Talk

When emperor penguins mate, they get together on land in big groups called colonies. The female lays one egg and then must leave to feed at sea. While she's away, it's the male's job to babysit the egg and keep it warm under a flap of skin near his feet. The mother can be gone for months, and during this time the father emperor penguin doesn't eat at all. He also has to live through a very cold winter and feed the chick when it hatches! When the mother finally returns, the father hands the chick over to her and then leaves to get food for himself. He sure must be hungry by then!

emperor penguins and chick

Chapter 6: Big-Billed Birds

bill of a brown pelican

Alrighty mates, let's fly on over and visit with some of the greatest birds around—the pelicans! Most of my bird friends and I are called brown pelicans. But there are also Dalmatian pelicans, white pelicans, Australian pelicans, pink-backed pelicans, and lots more! We're pretty big (for birds, that is), and we live all over the world. Come along, mate—we're going to meet the pelicans!

Here's the Scoop

Pelicans have a very large bill with an expandable pouch hanging underneath it. This pouch is very useful when it comes to catching our dinners! Pelicans live on coasts and make big plunge-dives into the water to get fish. With our huge pouches, we can catch large fish, or a bunch of smaller ones, in one big scoop. And we make a huge splash when we go into the water. *Sploosh!* Hey, that's fun!

brown pelican diving

Clowning Around!

Q: Why didn't the pelican pay for his dinner?

A: Because his *bill* was too big!

peach
sea star

We love Nigel, but he's a bit clumsy! Pelicans are such large and heavy birds, it's amazing that they can fly at all. But when they do, it's pretty impressive!

Australian pelican chick

peli-chicks!

Pelicans get together in big colonies to have their chicks. We make nests in trees, or even on the ground sometimes. I prefer the trees myself—better view, you know! After we make our nests out of big piles of branches, the females lay two or three eggs. When the chicks hatch out, their parents feed them by bringing back up partially digested food from that pouch under their bills. A pelican's pouch can hold more than twice as much as its stomach!

Something's Fishy

cormorant

Hey, kid! Have you ever eaten a rock? A bird called a cormorant does all the time! Cormorants are close relatives of pelicans. They actually swallow stones to help weigh themselves down so they can dive into the water better! Pretty heavy stuff, eh?

Chapter 7: Seagulls by the Seashore

 Hi, it's me Nemo again! Nigel's not a big fan of the next group of seabirds, so I told him I'd introduce you to them. Let's swim on over to Sydney Harbor and meet the seagulls.

A Seagull's Life

There are more than 50 different kinds of seagulls! They live along sandy coasts or rocky coasts with steep cliffs. Seagulls are usually white and have thick yellow bills. Like most seabirds, they have webbed feet to help them swim.

common seagull

Seafood for Seagulls

herring gull eating a fish head

Some kinds of seagulls are predators. That means they hunt for other animals to eat, like fish, shellfish, and even other birds! Other kinds of seagulls are scavengers. Scavengers search for food that's already dead, like fish that have washed up on the beach or leftovers from another animal's meal. They eat pretty much anything they can find. Scavenger seagulls even eat trash that people leave lying around.

GUll Greetings!

laughing gull

Laughing gulls live along the shores of North and South America. They usually steal food out of other birds' mouths. They might even steal food from a mighty pelican! That's why Nigel can't stand gulls—they can be pretty rude! Laughing gulls make a noise that sounds like "ha-ha-ha." My dad would love telling them jokes!

California gulls live along the west coast of North America. When they're ready to have chicks, they gather in huge groups of 2,000 to 40,000 birds! These gulls also seem to like games. They play together by dropping sticks and picking them up again!

California gull

great black-backed gull

Great black-backed gulls are the largest gulls of all! They live mostly along the coasts of Europe and North America. Black-backed gulls eat almost anything smaller than themselves, including small ducks, fish, shellfish, and eggs. In the winter, they eat a lot of fish that are driven up to the ocean's surface by humpback whales passing through.

CLOWNING AROUND!

Q: Why do seagulls live near the sea?

A: Because if they lived by the bay they would be called *bagels!*

Chapter 8: The BIGGEST Flying Bird of All

Albatrosses are some of the largest flying birds in the world. They can weigh more than 22 pounds (10 kg). That's a heavy bird! Albatrosses sure do love the ocean. They sleep on the sea surface, drink seawater, and eat fish, squid, and other small sea animals. Let's soar on over and take a look at these awesome albatrosses!

Spread Those Wings!

The wandering albatross has the largest wingspan of any bird. The length from one wing tip to the other is about 12 feet (3.7 m). That's longer than two average-sized adult humans lying head to head! Those super-large wings allow an albatross to fly great distances. Albatrosses can also glide on winds without flapping their wings a lot. This allows them to travel a long way without using too much energy. And this is important because they need to save energy for the journey back home!

wandering albatrosses

Big Babies

The only time albatrosses come onto land is when they raise their babies, or chicks. Then albatrosses get together on tiny islands in the middle of the ocean. Females lay just one large egg. It weighs about half a pound (0.23 kg). The albatross mother and father keep the egg warm in their nest for almost three months before it hatches.

albatross chick in its nest

Once the chick hatches, it's hungry! But sometimes albatross nests are far away from food. That's when those huge wings come in handy! Albatross parents fly thousands of miles in a single trip looking for food for themselves and for their chicks. Scientists who study birds think albatrosses only have one chick at a time because they have to do so much work to bring back food!

albatross caring for its chick

You've done some great learning about seabirds so far. Nice work! Are you ready to take a break? Let's swim on over to the next page for some Fishy Fun!

FISHY FUN: Bird Brain!

Hey, dude! It's time to show off your bird smarts! Circle the correct answer for each question below. Then figure out what a pelican's favorite snack is at the bottom of the page by filling in the numbered boxes (1–5) with the letter of each correct answer. If you need help, turn back to pages 23–24. Good luck! *(When you're done, check your answers on page 38.)*

1. What part of a bird helps it to scoop, spear, or catch its prey?
   - C. tail
   - F. beak or bill
   - W. eyes

2. What comes in many sizes and colors and helps a bird stay warm and protected?
   - B. neck
   - K. wings
   - I. feathers

3. What part of a bird allows it to fly from one place to another?
   - S. wings
   - N. webbed feet
   - A. head

4. What is located at the bottom of a bird and helps it to swim and paddle in the water?
   - O. beak or bill
   - E. feathers
   - H. webbed feet

5. What is the little organ that gathers salt in a seabird's body?
   - G. heart
   - Y. salt gland
   - I. lungs

Answer:

A | F | I | S | H | Y
1 | 2 | 3 | 4 | 5

SNACK!

SHOW·AND·TELL

with Ornithologist, Betty Anne Schreiber

We have a special guest at Undersea School! Her name is Betty Anne Schreiber. Betty Anne is an ornithologist (or-nith-AH-loh-jist), which means she's a scientist who studies birds. She works as a Research Associate at the National Museum of Natural History at the Smithsonian in Washington, DC. Are you ready to take flight with Betty Anne and learn some super-fun seabird facts? Let's go!

Why do you like to study seabirds?

BETTY ANNE: I like studying seabirds because watching their behavior is fascinating. They are not afraid of people and you can sit close to them and watch them. When I started studying seabirds, very little was known about them. There were many questions that we didn't know the answers to, questions like: Do they return to the same island each year to lay their eggs? How long do they live? How many chicks do they raise in their lifetime? With the research I've done, we've learned the answers to some of these questions.

What are some cool bird discoveries you've made in your research?

BETTY ANNE: When I started studying seabirds, many scientists believed that bird parents that didn't build a nest didn't stay with the same partner for life. Well, we soon found out this was wrong. A type of seabird called a masked booby does not build a nest, but over the years, I discovered that in general, masked booby partners or mates stay together for their entire lives!

masked booby

Where have you traveled to study seabirds?

BETTY ANNE: I have traveled all over the world. I've studied birds in Africa, South America, the Caribbean, and some of the islands in the Pacific Ocean.

What do you hope to discover in the future?

BETTY ANNE: I am working on a project that involves putting little electronic devices (like radios) on seabirds so I can find out where they go when they're not on the island where they raise their chicks.

Why are seabirds important to study?

BETTY ANNE: Seabirds can tell us a lot about the health of the ocean. By studying what they eat, where they live, and how they behave, we can learn about ocean pollution and how much food (like fish and squid) fishermen are taking out of the ocean.

What are some of your favorite seabirds?

BETTY ANNE: It's hard to say—they're all so interesting! I spend a lot of time studying birds called boobies, frigatebirds, tropicbirds, and terns. Comparing what they do and how they do it is fascinating!

white terns

School's Out!

I hope you had fun hanging out with all those totally awesome sea turtles, sea snakes, and seabirds. They really are cool, aren't they? We learned all about what these reptiles and birds eat, how they breathe air even while living in the ocean, how their bodies are specially adapted for swimming, and how they raise their babies. You've met a sea turtle that can swim 3,000 miles (4,828 km) and a penguin that's only one foot (30.5 cm) tall!

There's a lot more fun to come at Undersea School! We're going to be exploring the deepest and darkest depths of the ocean, checking out coral reefs, swimming to some of the coldest places on Earth, and doing lots of other cool stuff! See you next time!

> Nice flying with you, mate!

> That was a totally awesome adventure! Later, dude!

**Fishy Fun:
What's Wrong in
the Water?
(page 22)**

Did you find all
six strange things
in this underwater
scene?

**Fishy Fun:
Bird Brain! (page 35)**

You must be a
bird expert by
now! Here are the
answers to the
bird questions and
riddle...

1. **F.** beak or bill
2. **I.** feathers
3. **S.** wings
4. **H.** webbed feet
5. **Y.** salt gland

A **F** **I** **S** **H** **Y** SNACK!
  1   2   3   4   5